EVENTS
VERSUS
PROCESS

Paul Scanlon

Abundant Life Publishing

© Paul Scanlon 2005

Abundant Life Publishing
Wapping Road
Bradford
West Yorkshire
BD3 0EQ

Paul Scanlon has asserted his right under the Copyright, Designs and Patents Act, 1988, to be identified as Author of this work.

All rights reserved. No part of this publication may be reproduced, stored in a retrieval system, or transmitted, in any form or by any means, electronic, mechanical, photocopying, recording or otherwise, without the prior permission of the publisher or the Copyright Licensing Agency.

Unless otherwise stated, scripture quotations are from the Holy Bible, New International Version, Copyright © 1973, 1978, 1984 International Bible Society, published by Hodder and Stoughton.

First Published in 2005

Printed by:
Interprint Creative Solutions
Market Flat Lane
Knaresborough
North Yorkshire
HG5 9JA

www.interprint-ltd.co.uk

British Library Cataloguing in Publication Data
A catalogue record for this book is available from the British Library

ISBN 0-9538516-5-6

CONTENTS

Chapter 1
Spotting the Symptoms

Chapter 2
Maximising Events

Chapter 3
The Power of Process

Chapter 4
Supernatural Vs. Spectacular

Chapter 5
Foundational Choices

Introduction

This teaching is amongst the most important that I have ever done. It is of a fundamental and foundational nature. Foundational things by definition are below ground, out of sight and hidden. We assume the presence of foundations in the buildings around us because we see the buildings standing tall. But any weaknesses in them will be exposed over time either by an event like an earthquake or through a process of gradual subsidence. Then it's too late.

Introduction

I spent weeks developing this concept with my home church because I realised that people would not appreciate its value from a casual glance. By itself this teaching is not exciting, entertaining or eventful enough to command the attention it so deserves. It's like a quiet child amongst a boisterous family; it gets little attention because it doesn't shout the loudest. But I want to speak up for this quiet child and say to all the noisy attention-grabbing kids, 'Be quiet!' because this quiet child really does have something to say.

'God is committed to re-educating and moving his people from event based Christianity. Their fruitfulness and usefulness depends upon it!'

CHAPTER 1

Spotting The Symptoms

It never ceases to amaze me how when two people go through an identical experience they can be affected in such completely different ways. Take two guys with identical skills who are made redundant on the same day from the same job in the same company. Six months later one is depressed, distraught and bitter about being laid off. His redundancy money is spent. His life has been ruined by the company's decision. He believes he has no prospects; his working life is over; he is destined for the scrapheap of discarded former employees who scrape together an existence living off benefits and handouts.

CHAPTER 1 **Spotting The Symptoms**

His colleague, however, now has a new job. He has started a small business offering those same skills back to larger companies like the one who laid him off. They happily contract his services in for short contracts rather than employing full time staff to do the task. He reflects on being made redundant with a smile on his face and a glint in his eye; it was just the opportunity he needed. He had always wanted to start his own business and being made redundant was just the nudge he needed to take the risk and launch his business. In years to come, when he has made his first million, he will no doubt reflect back on his redundancy as just one small event in the process of his exciting business journey. His colleague however will still be parked up, bemoaning the event that ruined his life and just hoping that another positive event will enter his world from somewhere. But he's not holding his breath!

CHAPTER 1 **Spotting The Symptoms**

One man saw life as a process, the other man saw life as an event. What happened next was everything to do with their respective worldviews. One worked with each event in life and had the wisdom to stand back from it and see where it fitted into the process of his life. The other just saw the event; the event was his life and his life would not change unless another event entered his world.

Take two Christians who were saved on the same day, then attended the same conference and are now sat under the same preached Word of God. The preacher moves into a spontaneous time of ministering to the congregation and declares, 'God says there are a number of you here tonight who will be used mightily by me to reach the hurting people in your community. Go in my name and bind up their wounds as you have opportunity.' They each think to themselves, 'That was a Word from God for me; that is what I must do. I am called to reach the hurting in my community.'

'One man sees life as a process, another sees life as a series of random events'

CHAPTER 1 **Spotting The Symptoms**

One returns to his church and waits for an opportunity to appear that looks something like the fulfilment of the Word from God. Maybe the Pastor will initiate a new ministry he can join. He wonders what the opportunity will look like, but six months later nothing has happened. So he seeks God for clarity: 'Just what did you mean by hurting, Lord? What kind of hurt in particular? And what opportunity am I waiting for?' He decides to go to another conference with more of a prophetic emphasis in the hope that God will speak to him again. He goes forward for prayer and someone pronounces over him, 'The time is near; behold I see before you an open door to a time of fruitfulness and blessing, and from your blessing many shall drink and be satisfied.' Fantastic! Home he goes and waits for the door to open. Another few months go by and the pastor has still not started a new ministry which he feels is truly appropriate to that meant by God's Word to him.

CHAPTER 1   **Spotting The Symptoms**

He makes an appointment to see the Pastor. 'I will think about it' says the Pastor, 'But I am sure you could serve somewhere in the meantime. We have so much going on and many of the ministry teams need more volunteers, so I suggest you just get stuck in and help some people. Many of them are truly hurting!' This is not what he wants to hear. No, he is anticipating a specific door to open, it will be a door to a specific yet to be revealed hurting people-group, which will be so obviously a 'God thing' even the Pastor will realise it is the fulfilment of God's Word to him and invite him to lead it. So he returns to the pews. Years later he is still waiting for the event, his life on hold waiting for the clarification he seeks and the elusive door to open. He's been to a few other prophetic conferences too and each time felt affirmed in his decision to wait because 'it will happen soon'. And as he waits, the abused, damaged, hurting souls in his community bleed, mourn and die for want of the love, practical help and support he could have given.

CHAPTER 1 **Spotting The Symptoms**

Meanwhile our second Christian, Tom, returned from the conference all fired up. As he was parking his car he noticed his neighbour Joe in the garden.

'Hi Joe' he chirped.

'Oh, hi there' responded Joe but his tone was heavy.

'Is everything OK?' asked Tom.

'Well no, not really' said Joe. Tom noticed that his eyes were red; it looked as if he'd been crying.

'Anything I can help with?'

'Not really' said Joe. 'It's our son James. Keep this to yourself but we've found evidence of drugs in his room. So I confronted him about it yesterday and this morning we have found his room empty. He's gone, just like that! We feel so betrayed. I mean we have loved that boy like no other; he's always had what he wanted. You should see the state his mother is in… that's why I'm out here. This is just killing us.'

CHAPTER 1 **Spotting The Symptoms**

As the evening wore on Tom invited Joe and his wife round for a drink. The two couples chatted away, tears were shed and Tom and his wife were able to support and strengthen their hurting neighbours.

Later that night Tom told his wife about the conference and what God had said. But most importantly just how fantastic it was that God's Word had come true even before he got back into the house! Over the months following they were able to bind up the wounds of their hurting neighbours and this introduced them to a whole new world. They became aware of other families similarly ravaged by their children taking drugs. In response they approached their Pastor with a new ministry idea, a ministry that would have as its focus the support of families affected by drug using family members. They had already started it anyway! All the Pastor did was empower them, resource them and facilitate their vision which then attracted other like-minded people. In time a thriving ministry was 'healing the hurting' in their community.

CHAPTER 1 **Spotting The Symptoms**

Spot the difference! Our first Christian saw life as a series of events devoid of process. He needed another conference event and for his Pastor to create an event-like opportunity for him. His whole life was spent waiting for the next event. Whereas Tom lived his life as a process, each day's events simply contributed to the process of living life in step with the Holy Spirit. He worked *with* God in a process rather than waiting *for* God to send the next event.

Time For Detox

These two worldviews each came from somewhere. They have roots into family life, education, relationships and church life. But like many things in the Christian life, it is sometimes easier to spot the symptoms than the root cause. Based on the symptoms I am describing I would simply call the root conditions *'Event based Christianity'* and *'Process based Christianity'* respectively. One describes Christians who live from event to event; the other describes Christians who live life as a process.

CHAPTER 1 **Spotting The Symptoms**

God wants the latter. He wants you to live life as a process in harmony with him. He wants every event, however good or bad, to find its place in that relational process. In fact, God is committed to re-educating and moving his people from event based Christianity to process based Christianity. Their fruitfulness and usefulness depends upon it!

At the heart of what many of you reading this are currently going through, is a transition orchestrated by God to move you from an event based Christianity to a process based Christianity. The insecurity, uncertainty, fear and panic that you sometimes feel is a kind of spiritual 'cold turkey' as you withdraw from your event dependency habit. It's time to admit that you have an events addiction, you are an 'events junkie' and the longer you go between 'hits' the more strung out you become. The 'pushers' who supply your addiction are the 'quick fix' preachers - and at times I have been one of them - who promise

CHAPTER 1 **Spotting The Symptoms**

you an instant breakthrough for everything you don't want to deal with through a process. Their context is this quick-fix 21st century western culture in which we live. This 'spirit of the age' elevates and celebrates instantaneous events and barely tolerates slow moving process.

Please understand, I'm all for getting things done faster and more efficiently wherever possible. But the truth is that some things

> 'This "spirit of the age" elevates and celebrates instantaneous events and barely tolerates slow moving process.'

take time and that's OK. Process says: 'things don't happen in a day, things develop daily'.

Dangerous Overestimation

Because of the events based worldview we are raised in, we tend to overestimate the conference, the prophecy, the preaching and the prayer line. We tell ourselves that the more dramatic the event, the bigger

'Events are good for making decisions but only process can bring lasting change'

CHAPTER 1 **Spotting The Symptoms**

the result will be. I thank God for events, for every touch, blessing, encounter and miracle. But events without process will not produce lasting change.

During the past thirty years, which I have spent in the same local church, I have all too often witnessed people over endorsing the ability of an event to change their life. Sadly, weeks or even just days later, the enemy cashes in on their unreality as they battle disillusionment and disappointment because the problem still exists. What I have tried to teach people is that the event was good for making a decision, a commitment, a stand, but that decision will not bring about the desired change without the back up of a process. Events are good for making decisions but only process can bring lasting change.

When we look to an event for things that can come only by process, we create a life of false expectations. Events become loaded with such high expectations that if the event could speak I'm sure it would say,

CHAPTER 1   **Spotting The Symptoms**

'I'm only an event! I can help you make some decisions but those decisions will take time to work out. You need to meet my close friend process, we always work together'.

Therefore, don't build your life primarily on event based decisions or experiences, build your life on process. Don't rely on events to change, move or convict you, instead commit to a life-long process of growing and changing.

Fruitful Life or Eventful Life?

I trust that you are getting to grips with the concept I want to explore in this book. As you can see, it is very fundamental to the way we live our Christian life and particularly to our fruitfulness. In fact I would even go so far as to say that you can only really have one or the other, a fruitful life or an eventful life. And I know which I want! Let me illustrate it from the following words of Jesus:

CHAPTER 1 **Spotting The Symptoms**

'Watch out for false prophets. They come to you in sheep's clothing, but inwardly they are ferocious wolves. By their fruit you will recognize them. Do people pick grapes from thorn bushes, or figs from thistles? Likewise, every good tree bears good fruit, but a bad tree bears bad fruit. A good tree cannot bear bad fruit, and a bad tree cannot bear good fruit. Every tree that does not bear good fruit is cut down and thrown into the fire. Thus, by their fruit you will recognize them.

Not everyone who says to me, "Lord, Lord," will enter the kingdom of heaven, but only he who does the will of my Father who is in heaven. Many will say to me on that day, "Lord, Lord, did we not prophesy in your name, and in your name drive out demons and perform many miracles?" Then I will tell them plainly, "I never knew you. Away from me, you evildoers!"'[1]

> 'God is not looking for an eventful life, he is looking for a fruitful life'

CHAPTER 1 **Spotting The Symptoms**

Here we see the difference between people who live their lives in a consistent process of fruit bearing and those who bypass the process in favour of momentous events, believing that they will achieve a certain outcome. Jesus fast-forwards the consequences of both lives to their ultimate conclusion. His response to those who expected entrance to heaven based on events they had performed, like prophesying, casting out demons or performing miracles was, 'I never knew you'. But those who had outworked 'the will of my Father' in a process of consistent fruitfulness would 'enter the kingdom of heaven'.

A tree is known by what it bears and fruit bearing is a process not an event. The message is clear: events can never replace process. In fact life doesn't have to be either/or, it can be an awesome combination of both. God is not looking for an eventful life, he is looking for a fruitful life.

CHAPTER 1   **Spotting The Symptoms**

Awesome Combinations

The more we understand the differences between events and process based Christianity, the better equipped we will be to spot the symptoms and adjust accordingly. This is the kind of principle that once you have understood it, you will see it everywhere! Before long you will be seeing your life as one awesome combination of a process interspersed by a series of events.

For example, you succeed in something; you pass an exam, gain a promotion or accomplish an ambition. Was it an event or a process? An event most definitely; it happened on a certain day at a certain time and just thinking about it makes you smile and your adrenaline rise. But that promotion was the result of three years hard work - a process! That exam success was the result of two years of study - a process! The ambition you accomplished may have taken years

CHAPTER 1 **Spotting The Symptoms**

to plan, save, train and sacrifice for – a process! And what's more, the success you have achieved must now be sustained by a further process of hard work. The combination of an ongoing process and the event builds you a successful life. And if you experience a failure along the way, it too finds its place in the process and never becomes an event you 'park on' for the rest of your life.

A successful life is therefore a process, not just a successful event. In the same way, a failed life is a process and never the result of a single failed event.

Debt is a Process

Is debt a process or an event? Again it can be viewed as both; a single debt does not mean you are a life-long debtor, it is an event. But if you become known as a debtor because it characterises your whole life and controls you, a process has been at work.

'The combination of an ongoing process and the event builds you a successful life.'

CHAPTER 1 **Spotting The Symptoms**

When Glenda and I were raising our young family, we once accumulated a significant debt on a credit card. Eventually its size began to influence our spending decisions. We could not give because of the debt, we could not be as generous as we would have liked to be because of it and frankly, our family were suffering because if it. We had to face up to it and deal with it. But how? Pray for debt cancellation? That would have been some event! No, we had to work a process. In fact it took us the best part of three years to restrict our spending elsewhere and deliberately pay the debt off. Eventually we got free because we were determined not to let this event shape our lives but worked it through in a process that led to our prosperity.

With hindsight I see more than ever that this was a negative event which we took control of and allowed to shape a bigger, positive, life-sized process.

CHAPTER 1   ***Spotting The Symptoms***

Today we are prospering, but this is in no small part the result of learning from a series of related events. We learned to deal with debt, we learned to be givers, we learned to be generous, to sow and reap, to give cheerfully and that we can never out-give God. Each lesson was an event, and some were painful, but the overall process is what we were working on. The events and the process together have been a powerful combination that has shaped our lives.

Think for a moment of Christian friends you particularly admire; people who have stood the test of time, grown in grace and worked through bad as well as good times. People who seem to have a lot in the bank spiritually speaking, yet are still growing, learning and doing things for God. Why are they like that? Because they are living their whole Christian lives as a process that involves 'being transformed

CHAPTER 1 **Spotting The Symptoms**

into his likeness with ever-increasing glory'.[2] No event, be it positive or negative, has been allowed to dominate their spiritual development; no prophecy, no encounter with God, no lapse of integrity, no error of judgment or miracle they performed. Each was simply integrated into the process of their Christian life and what you see today is the kind of believer you would like to be, one living a 'process based Christianity'.

Even the greatest of events may not significantly shape your life unless you are working on the process. I heard recently of a man who had literally been raised from the dead following the prayer of believing relatives. His testimony became well known, after all, what an event! But today he is backslidden and away from God. Why? Because however momentous the events

> 'Even the greatest of events may not significantly shape your life unless you are working on the process.'

CHAPTER 1   **Spotting The Symptoms**

in your life, they will only enrich your whole life as part of a process. Sadly, he was not working a process of following God as a life-style and with a whole heart. If he had been, the impact of his testimony could have been awesome. But to be truly awesome every event needs to be working in combination with a positive process.

Wilderness Warning

The New Testament writers urge us to learn from the example of God's people Israel in the Old Testament. On one occasion Paul says, *'These things happened to them as examples and were written down as warnings for us, on whom the fulfillment of the ages has come. So, if you think you are standing firm, be careful that you don't fall!'*[3] He was referring particularly to the fact that they had travelled from Egypt to the borders of the Promised Land and then failed to go in and enjoy it.

CHAPTER 1 **Spotting The Symptoms**

Just think about their story. There was a process at work, the process of God redeeming his people from slavery in Egypt to live in the fullness of their inheritance in Canaan; a story that mirrors many aspects of our Christian journey from sin's bondage to living a fulfilling Christian life. Yet each day was also an event. The manna appeared for breakfast and the quails flew in for evening meal; their clothes did not wear out and they were supernaturally guided and protected by the pillar of cloud and fire. Each day was an incredibly supernatural event! But they did not enter their land. Why? Because they were living a form of 'event based Christianity'. They enjoyed the events but did not grasp the part they were supposed to play in their more important life-process. As a result, when faced with the prospect of displacing the occupying enemy, they pulled back in unbelief. They halted the process and found themselves stuck in a 'ground hog day' event which,

CHAPTER 1　**Spotting The Symptoms**

though supernatural, was not their destiny and they died in the wilderness.

I'm sure that like me, you are now beginning to realise just how fundamental an issue this is for our Christian growth and fruitfulness. So, having explained something of how to spot the basic symptoms of 'event based Christianity' and 'process based Christianity' respectively, we will now dig a little deeper into our daily management of the life-shaping relationship between events and process.

---

[1] Matthew 7:15-23
[2] 2 Corinthians 3:18
[3] 1 Corinthians 10:11-12

'To be truly awesome every event needs to be working in combination with a positive process'

'However momentous the events in your life, they will only enrich your whole life as part of a process'

CHAPTER 2

Maximising Events

One day Jesus came across a man who had been crippled for 38 years.[1] He was waiting by a pool for an event that would change his life. He got his event, albeit in a different way to that which he had been expecting. Later on he encountered Jesus again and at this second meeting Jesus said something very personal to him: *'See, you are well again. Now stop sinning or something worse may happen to you.'* [2] In other words, unless you follow through after your miraculous event with a new lifestyle, a new process, you may lose the benefit of the event.

CHAPTER 2 **_Maximising Events_**

Again, when describing what happens when a demon is cast out of a person, Jesus contrasted events with process: *'When an evil spirit comes out of a man, it goes through arid places seeking rest and does not find it. Then it says, "I will return to the house I left." When it arrives, it finds the house swept clean and put in order. Then it goes and takes seven other spirits more wicked than itself, and they go in and live there. And the final condition of that man is worse than the first.'*[3]

> 'Unless you follow through after your miraculous event with a new lifestyle, a new process, you may lose the benefit of the event.'

Like any successful intruder, the demon returns to the last house he robbed just in case the owners haven't bothered to improve security. When the return visit reveals that the event of deliverance has become a swept clean, beautifully preserved show house instead of a re-occupied home, he moves back in with others. The event of casting

CHAPTER 2   *Maximising Events*

the demon out was not enough without the process of a new way of life to back it up. Then when that demon came sniffing around again, he would find the house filled with new burglar-proof systems in the form of new values, truths, habits, relationships and culture.

To Keep The Event, Start a Process

These examples from Jesus teach us that if we want to keep the event and all the potential it carries, we must start a process. Of course the ideal situation is that there is already a process in place. But the truth is that many Christians have lived from event to event for so long that they have to initiate a new one. They have to make a conscious decision to begin working with God in a long-term process, which requires resolve, commitment and perseverance.

I have often noted that Christians who are transitioning from 'event based Christianity' to 'process based

CHAPTER 2 **Maximising Events**

Christianity' start well. They have an initial surge of enthusiasm and determine to live each day as part of a life-long process of growth and development with God. Early events are quickly integrated into their life-process. Negative events do not hijack them like they used to; instead they press through and allow the event to enrich the process of their lives. Similarly, positive events are not over endorsed and camped upon for too long. And so the process continues.

But this is a life-long process. And somewhere along the way your willingness to trust God with the whole process gets tested. Even though you have started to live a process based Christian life, your old desire for an event to speed things up can become your downfall.

I am mindful of Abraham to whom God said, *'Leave your country, your people and your father's household and go to the land I will show you. I will make you into a great nation and I will bless you; I will make your name*

CHAPTER 2 **Maximising Events**

great, and you will be a blessing. I will bless those who bless you, and whoever curses you I will curse; and all peoples on earth will be blessed through you.'[4] This was a life-sized promise that demanded a life-sized process to see it through to fulfillment. And Abraham was up for it. We read in the very next verse, *'So Abram left, as the LORD had told him.*'[5] He started a process. Like many of us, he started well.

The process, however, required a son and heir through whom the promise could be fulfilled and this was long in coming. Abraham and Sarah needed the event of a pregnancy and fast! After all, they were getting on in years and were technically 'past it' when it came to having children. They would need a miracle, which was of course another event God would have to initiate. And so they waited, living each day as a process but becoming increasingly desperate for that one event they knew was crucial to their success. This was their test.

'To keep the benefit of an event, you must follow it up with a process'

CHAPTER 2 **Maximising Events**

Sadly they failed by creating an event. They in effect tried to help God out because it seemed he was not moving the process on as quickly as he should have been! The result was the birth of Ishmael, an event that grieved God and created a major problem in their family household.[6] A close reading of the text also reveals that after this event God did not speak to Abraham again for thirteen years; the daily process and their developing relational walk had been hijacked by forcing an event into it.

Thirteen years later, in God's good time, he spoke to Abraham again, confirmed that his original promise still stood and that its fulfillment was near. The seal of this was to be circumcision and on that same day Abraham and Ishmael were both circumcised – Abraham was ninety nine and Ishmael aged thirteen.[7]

The event of Ishmael's birth was eventually integrated into the process of Abraham's life. It cost him dearly

CHAPTER 2 **Maximising Events**

but also enriched him. He was wiser for it but could really have done without it! Such is the nature of forcing events into a process once we have started it.

It is worth noting that soon after this, Isaac was born. His birth was an event in its proper time; it left no bad taste as it too was integrated into the progressive process of Abraham's life. So, Abraham actually kept things in his life from both birth events, some good and some bad. The most important thing to see is that both only found their place and could yield their lessons and enrich his life because he had been courageous enough to start the process in the first place. He then pressed through the trauma of the Ishmael event, sailed through the Isaac event with joy and camped on neither. To do so would have thwarted the process of his life.

CHAPTER 2 ***Maximising Events***

The potential for you and I to do the same is an everyday reality. And for this reason I am appealing through the pages of this book for an absolute commitment to 'process based Christianity'. We then keep all the lessons and benefits of the daily events of our lives without any of them dominating the process and hindering its progress… assuming of course that you have actually started the process!

Where Process Starts

'What came first, the chicken or the egg?' Asks the age-old conundrum. And our subject is not unlike it because in the context of living your Christian life, 'What came first, the event or the process?'

The answer given will teach you something about your world-view. If you immediately think of the event of your salvation moment, you may well have lived 'event based Christianity' ever since. But if you

CHAPTER 2　**Maximising Events**

immediately thought of the process of searching that led you to a salvation encounter and which has since continued in a relationship process with God, you are probably living 'process based Christianity'.

I think that many Christians live from event to event because of the way they started their Christian life. It was an event and no one can deny it; it was the most momentous event of your human existence. And whether you acknowledge the presence of a progressive process in your life before you came to Christ, you certainly have to admit that this life-changing event was intended to be the start of a new life-process.

Wherever people are not living their lives as a process, it usually takes an event to kick-start one – just like your salvation. Process has to start somewhere and a significant event is no bad starting place as long as the relationship between the event and the process is understood as we have been explaining.

CHAPTER 2 **Maximising Events**

Going to a conference can be a process kick-starting moment. In the unfamiliar setting you are more open to God; you attended for a reason and were anticipating an encounter, a word, a flash of revelation, or something to strengthen your life. And when it comes the important thing is that you leave that conference determined never to have to revisit that moment again; from here on you are going to outwork God's direction to you as a process.

A prayer of healing or deliverance can be another process kick-starting moment. You responded to an appeal for ministry or maybe requested prayer from your church leaders. Their prayer became a trigger for your faith and God met you. You walked away free from that which bound you. And most importantly you quietly determined in your heart that you would never again allow yourself to be bound by that thing; you left determined to live free and to never have to seek an event like that again.

CHAPTER 2 **Maximising Events**

I think that every event is supposed to either motivate us to start a process or simply be integrated into the already existing one. And where no process exists, God is particularly good to us in sending events which school us to trust him as part of a process.

It is interesting to note how God led his people in the period between leaving Egypt and their entry to the Promised Land. Think for a moment: who actually led them? Was it Moses or the cloud? Initially it was the cloud; God himself intervened and led them out of Egypt and into the desert – quite an event! The cloud became their guide; when it moved so did they. The cloud also represented God amongst his people and whenever God spoke to Moses the cloud was present, hiding Holy God from sinful humanity. But there was a greater purpose at work in all this. When God met Moses on the mountain, the cloud

> 'And where no process exists, God is particularly good to us in sending events which school us to trust him as part of a process.'

'The good news is that any event can become the motivational starting point of a new life-process'

CHAPTER 2 **Maximising Events**

covered it. When God spoke to Moses from the Tent of Meeting, the cloud came down and covered it. Why? Because God was schooling the people to trust the leadership of Moses as a daily process and weaning them off a reliance on the event of the cloud appearing. God made this clear when he said to Moses: *'I am going to come to you in a dense cloud, so that the people will hear me speaking with you and will always put their trust in you.'*[8] God was pleased to lead them through events initially but wanted them to settle into a process based walk with him that involved trusting the daily leadership of Moses.

I wonder what events God has used in your life to kick-start a process of daily walking with him? Maybe you didn't even realise this was what God was wanting for you and have therefore drifted into 'event based Christianity.' The good news is that any events like these can become the motivational starting point of a new life-process. Sure, it was an event. But what matters is that it found its place in the process of

CHAPTER 2 **Maximising Events**

your life and you now move forward making steady daily progress in your process of walking with God. You are living 'process based Christianity' and it all started with an event.

Not Always an Event

Yet process does not always start with an event! Have you ever met people who have trouble telling you about any significant events in their lives yet still seem to be growing, changing and doing great things for God? Their lives shout 'process' but they are not too sure where it started because they are not particularly event conscious.

This is also true of churches. I am frequently asked by other church leaders for the keys to building a thriving church like the one I am privileged to lead. And I am left scratching my head thinking, 'I am not sure how to answer that'. Why? Because as I look back there are very few events that have shaped our journey, events that provided outstanding keys to

CHAPTER 2   **Maximising Events**

> 'Commitment to the process, the journey, the long haul is what builds a great church, in just the same way as it builds a great personal life.'

growth and momentum. All we have done is walked with God one day at a time, one step at a time in a process. Each day we have tweaked church structures, our staffing, ministry programmes and relationships. Each day we have sought to be obedient, worked on our attitudes and characters, acted quickly to God's voice and implemented a myriad of small changes as appropriate. So I look back at a path strewn with footprints! Each day was a small step in the process of our growth and development. And I think this should be the norm. Commitment to the process, the journey, the long haul is what builds a great church, in just the same way as it builds a great personal life.

As you cultivate a 'process based Christianity' you will find yourself making decisions easily and without a big fuss – they don't become an event! You decide

CHAPTER 2   *Maximising Events*

to train for a qualification, to finish with your girlfriend, to move house, to involve in a new ministry and just get on with it as part of the process. You no longer need 'angels river-dancing on the duvet' or three prophecies and a poem to confirm that this is a good decision. Your life is about the process not the event. And before too long you will find yourself qualified, married, settled in a home, busy in ministry and living a fulfilled and fruitful life. 'How did you do it?' some will ask. And you will reflect back and say, 'I don't know really; just one step at a time; it's just been a process!'

Maximised Events

What we have established in this chapter is that events do have a place. They can be amazing bringers of impetus to our lives and have the power to kick-start us into a life of fruitful process. But most importantly, I want you to understand that to maximise

CHAPTER 2 **Maximising Events**

all that an event contains and can add to your life, it must be integrated into a process.

I thank God for every encounter I have had with him, every significant life-shaping word, every triumph and disaster, because they have all been events that have contributed to me being the person I am today. Yet I remain convinced that if I had the same experiences without my deep commitment to a life of process, their impact would have been far less or far worse, and I would be the lesser for it. To maximise your events they must be part of an ongoing process.

---

[1] John 5:1-8
[2] John 5:14
[3] Luke 11:24-26
[4] Genesis 12:1-3
[5] Genesis 12:4
[6] Genesis 16
[7] Genesis 16:16, 17:1, 17:24-26
[8] Exodus 19:9

'How did you do it?' some will ask. And you will reflect back and say, 'I don't know really; just one step at a time; it's just been a process!'

'This is a sobering truth; process is far more powerful than any single event and as such we must be sure to observe the processes of life and not get overly caught up in the events'

CHAPTER 3

The Power of Process

'*S*how us a sign and we will believe' is what the religious leaders of Jesus' day demanded. They wanted him to do something sufficiently miraculous to convince them of who he was. Jesus' reply once again sprang from his appeal to the power of process: *'The mood of this age is all wrong - everybody's looking for proof, but you're looking for the wrong kind. All you're looking for is something to titillate your curiosity, satisfy your lust for miracles, but the only proof you're gonna get is the Jonah proof given to the Ninevites, which looks like no proof at all. But what Jonah was to Nineveh, I am to this age.'* [1]

CHAPTER 3 **The Power of Process**

In other words, people who refuse to see what's obvious and instead ask for a sign - an event - are often avoiding their responsibility of dealing with what they already know to be true. Jesus pointed to the process of God's multiple attempts to reach out to people throughout history. He was simply informing them that the process of Jonah's preaching was the only sign that Nineveh got and that his preaching would be the only sign the Jews would get. If that was more than enough for the Ninevites who had far less of a messenger than Jesus, then they had no grounds to ask for some weird and wonderful sign or event from him now.

Jesus made the same point when he told the story of the rich man and Lazarus. In the after life the rich man, now in hell, is trying to convince Abraham that the dramatic event of Lazarus returning from the dead to warn his family would save them from a similar fate. The conversation that followed is very informative:

CHAPTER 3 **The Power of Process**

'Abraham replied, "They have Moses and the Prophets; let them listen to them."

"No, father Abraham," he said, "but if someone from the dead goes to them, they will repent."

He said to him, "If they do not listen to Moses and the Prophets, they will not be convinced even if someone rises from the dead." ' [2]

The rich man wanted a dramatic event to grab the attention of his unbelieving relatives but Abraham pointed to the powerful testimony of process as sufficient information and opportunity to make men accountable regarding eternity. This is a sobering truth; process is far more powerful than any single event and as such we must be sure to observe the processes of life and not get overly caught up in the events.

CHAPTER 3 **The Power of Process**

Creation Speaks

The Apostle Paul was also well used to people demanding a sign to prove God's existence and in his teaching, pointed to another ongoing process that leaves people without excuse when it comes to believing in the existence, presence, power and nature of the invisible God: *'The wrath of God is being revealed from heaven against all the godlessness and wickedness of men who suppress the truth by their wickedness, since what may be known about God is plain to them, because God has made it plain to them. For since the creation of the world God's invisible qualities – his eternal power and divine nature – have been clearly seen, being understood from what has been made, so that men are without excuse.'*[3]

God doesn't refer to an event to establish man's accountability to believe in him but to the ongoing process of the created order, which Paul says makes God plain enough to people, so much so that they

CHAPTER 3 **The Power of Process**

are without excuse. He would no doubt have had the words of David the Psalmist at the back of his mind who wrote:

'The heavens declare the glory of God;
the skies proclaim the work of his hands.
Day after day they pour forth speech;
night after night they display knowledge.
There is no speech or language
where their voice is not heard.
Their voice goes out into all the earth,
their words to the ends of the world.'[4]

> 'The ongoing process of creation is sufficient evidence of an omnipotent creator.'

The interesting thing about Paul's writing is that even though he is writing to Christians in a post-crucifixion era, he doesn't centre mankind's accountability for believing in God exclusively on an awareness of the Cross. The ongoing process of creation is sufficient evidence of an omnipotent creator; the Cross of Calvary is the event through which that creator can be known personally.

'The purpose of the process of creation is to escort humanity to the event of Calvary'

CHAPTER 3 **The Power of Process**

The purpose of the process of creation is to escort humanity to the event of Calvary. At Calvary both God the creator, the God of process, and God the saviour, the God of divine intervention and rescue, came together perfectly. Sometimes process leads us to an event, sometimes it takes us onwards from an event. Either way, process must be the leader of our lives, not events.

Adam Missed Creation

The greatest six-day event of all time was completely missed by Adam the first man. Adam woke up into process, into a world that was already fruitful and reproductive. The fact is that God could have created Adam earlier if it had been appropriate. He could have made sure that Adam witnessed him speaking everything into being, but he didn't. It would seem that being present during the eventful days of creation was not essential to Adam's revelation and understanding of God.

CHAPTER 3 **The Power of Process**

This establishes an important principle regarding the way God wants us to relate to him. Adam's relationship with God was not based on events, God doing specific things for him or meeting his particular needs, but rather on process. Adam woke up into a world in process and was required to flow right into it. Consequently, he *'walked with God'*[5] as a process of everyday living, he didn't meet up with him every night in a prayer line! Adam talked with God on an ongoing basis, not just when he had a problem or specific need. Adam partnered with God in the process of naming the animals, caring for the garden and ultimately with Eve in the process of populating the earth.

> 'Adam's relationship with God was not based on events.'

Adam and Eve's mandate was processional and generational. They were to *'Be fruitful and increase in number; fill the earth and subdue it. Rule over the fish of the sea and the birds of the air and over every living*

'God started the way he intended things to go on. He intended his people to work with him in a life-long process of fruitfulness, multiplication, increase and dominion'

CHAPTER 3   *The Power of Process*

creature that moves on the ground.'[6] Their dominion mandate was progressive and to be passed on to successive generations. Continuity and process was built in right from the start. As far as we know Adam never performed a miracle, had a miraculous intervention in his life, saw a miracle or ever asked for one. He operated entirely according to cause and effect, sowing and reaping, obedience and blessing, action and reaction. His whole life was about the process.

I believe that God started the way he intended things to go on. He intended his people to work with him in a life-long process of fruitfulness, multiplication, increase and dominion. We could learn a lot from Adam's relationship with God.

Counselling From Process

As we have established, events have their place as

CHAPTER 3 *The Power of Process*

initiators of a process, as decision making points along the way and as much needed kick-starts at certain times in life. But all the true power is in the process.

One aspect of the pastoral ministry which highlights these issues most acutely is that of the counselling process. Over the years I have often wrestled with what seemed like a huge difference between my approach to a problem and the approach of those I was attempting to help through counselling. I didn't always understand what that gap was but I was very aware of its consequences. Some people became impatient and frustrated with my counsel, others had a kind of faked interest as if humouring me or being polite, yet had no real intention of changing. As a result I became weary of fighting to save the families, marriages and finances of people who were seemingly unwilling to fight for them themselves.

CHAPTER 3 **_The Power of Process_**

Exploring the issues in this book has helped me to understand that the gap was created by the difference between our two approaches to life. Because I am a firm believer that it's not life's problems which defeat us, it's who we are and how we think that defeats us, I counselled into the processes that had made them who they were. I tried to help them spot trends,

> 'It's not life's problems which defeat us, it's who we are and how we think that defeats us.'

mind-sets and attitudes that had contributed to the process of their lives and produced the so-called event they were describing as debt, irretrievable relationship breakdown or family break up. The problems they faced were simply exposing what was in them. I would then appeal to them for a process based response, a willingness to work at things long-term. But the more I explained both the process that caused the problems and the process that would resolve them, the more switched

CHAPTER 3 *The Power of Process*

off and disinterested they became. Why? Because I wasn't giving them an event as a quick-fix solution. I was counselling from a 'process based Christianity perspective' but they were listening from an 'events based Christianity' perspective. So, I was urging them towards a process while they were looking for me to conjure up a life saving event for them.

Raising great children is a process not an event. Treating the children occasionally just does not do it! How can a Disneyland event ever replace the parenting process? Yet many try to make it do so and then cry in despair when their relationship with their children goes sour. 'But we spent so much on them' goes the cry, 'We even took them to Disneyland and bought them expensive presents!' So what! As parents we have to be committed to a daily process of nurturing, training, disciplining, boundary setting, relationship building and all the joys and tears that go with it. It is a process, a powerful process, a

CHAPTER 3 **_The Power of Process_**

process that carries a great promise to Christian parents: *'Train a child in the way he should go, and when he is old he will not turn from it'*.[7] All the power is in the process. But if you get the chance to take the kids to Disneyland, go for it and have a blast! It will enrich the process of your parenting but can never replace it.

> 'Marriages fail because of events, they succeed because of commitment to process.'

Building a great marriage is a process not an event. The wedding day is an event, but that is all. It can be a very special event but as we have seen, to be truly purposeful it has to be solidly placed within a life-process. So, the engaged couple prepare for the event but actually they are preparing in a process for a bigger process that will commence the day after the wedding, it is called married life! Marriages fail because of events, they succeed because of commitment to process. The power is in the process.

CHAPTER 3   **The Power of Process**

Businesses thrive because of a commitment to process. The launch event comes and goes; the popularity of your product rises then falls. Then what? The process says diversify for growth, refinance for sustainable productivity, restructure for optimum efficiency, train your staff for new technologies, develop a long-term marketing strategy. Then process says, we can survive and prosper. The power is in working the process not an elaborate fancy launch event.

And so it is with individual lives and churches. I succeed as I continue to work with God in the process of change, becoming more and more like Jesus. Churches advance God's kingdom and grow as they commit to a process of being 'life saving stations', to being salt and light in society, to being relevant to their culture and having a credible testimony in their community.

All the power is in the process.

CHAPTER 3 ***The Power of Process***

---

[1] Luke 11:29 Message Bible
[2] Luke 16:19-31
[3] Romans 1:18-20
[4] Psalm 19:1-4
[5] Genesis 3:8
[6] Genesis 1:28
[7] Proverbs 22:6

'I succeed as I continue to work with God in the process of change, becoming more and more like Jesus'

'All the power is in the process'

CHAPTER 4

Supernatural Vs. Spectacular

As I have explored the differences between 'event based Christianity' and 'process based Christianity', I have become increasingly aware of one particular evidence of the imbalance between the two. This is seen in the confusion that exists between the supernatural and the spectacular in much of the church today.

It works like this: in an effort to speed up the spiritual process that God is taking us through, we look for an event. But not just any event, we want something really spectacular that will have the power to propel us a long way down the road of our spiritual growth.

CHAPTER 4 **_Supernatural Vs. Spectacular_**

We seek the spectacular rather than the naturally supernatural process of the Christian life. As a result we become confused; we come to associate supernatural events only with spectacular interventions by God. So, if we are not enjoying a spectacular encounter we cease to believe we are truly spiritual. This sends us on the hunt for such an encounter and inevitably leads us to the miracle conference, the prayer line and any interventionist style ministry which promises a spectacular quick fix.

I do not believe it is right to associate the supernatural only with the spectacular things God does. If you think about it, once we are born again we become supernatural people. We are back in relationship with the supernatural God who created us in his likeness, the God who loved us and saved us. He now wants us to walk in a daily relationship with him, a process which is fundamentally supernatural.

'The truth is that if you never have a single spectacular event in your Christian life, you can still live an awesome, supernatural life'

CHAPTER 4   **Supernatural Vs. Spectacular**

The Bible teaches that the Christian life is one of faith *'from first to last'*.[1] Faith is the essence of Christianity. Faith is *'being sure of what we hope for and certain of what we do not see'*,[2] it is the absolute conviction that what God says, he will do. Faith is so 'certain' that you can step out on it, which is what we do each and every day as we walk with God in the process of our Christian life.

Now think: is faith supernatural or spectacular? For the most part it is a supernatural process, a daily trusting in God as you take each step of your Christian life. Then, less frequently, God graciously intervenes in our lives with a more dramatic expression of his power through spectacular events. The truth is that if you never have a single spectacular event in your Christian life, you can still live an awesome, supernatural life which bears great fruit and makes a great impact.

CHAPTER 4   *Supernatural Vs. Spectacular*

Elijah's Adjustment

This was a lesson one of the most spectacular prophets of the Old Testament had to learn. Elijah was a true spiritual giant, a man of stature in his generation. No one would have ever accused him of not being supernatural. Yet even he had to learn that a supernatural life is a process not an event.

After the spectacular events of the contest between Elijah and the prophets of Baal on Mount Carmel,[3] Elijah received some news from the Baal worshipping Queen Jezebel: *'Jezebel sent a messenger to Elijah to say, "May the gods deal with me, be it ever so severely, if by this time tomorrow I do not make your life like that of one of them."'* [4] Not good news! But no less than he should have expected after having just killed 400 of them.[5] This had been a crucial contest, one which was establishing for his generation who the true God was, one designed to halt their wavering 'between two opinions'.[6] It was truly spectacular.

CHAPTER 4 *Supernatural Vs. Spectacular*

So, how was he to respond to this threat? Surely the God who had sent fire from heaven followed by torrential rain was great enough to deal with Jezebel. You wouldn't have thought so by his reaction: We read that *'Elijah was afraid and ran for his life. When he came to Beersheba in Judah, he left his servant there'*.[7] Beersheba was the southernmost town in Israel, right on the edge of the desert. He then traveled on into the desert for another forty days. His fear drove him a long way! Eventually he stopped and God spoke to him: *'What are you doing here?'*[8] asked God. After Elijah had bemoaned his situation, expressed his fear and depression, God spoke to him. But not in the spectacular mighty rushing wind that broke rocks, or the earthquake that followed it, or even in the more familiar fire from heaven which followed that – each were spectacular but *'God was not in them'*.[9] Then God spoke *'in a gentle whisper'*[10] and told Elijah what to do.

'That gentle whisper was the voice of process. It nudged him back into the process of his destiny and that was truly supernatural. Elijah's life did not need to be spectacular all the time'

CHAPTER 4 *Supernatural Vs. Spectacular*

That gentle whisper was the voice of process. It was God schooling Elijah that all he had to do was live each day listening to that whisper in his heart and respond accordingly. It nudged him back into a process of life that was truly supernatural and did not need to be spectacular all the time.

The content of God's instructions to him are also worth noting. He first told him to *'Go back the way you came'*.[11] Thus getting him back to the place that he ran from in search of a spectacular encounter. It got him back to the unfolding process of his life. Then he was to go and anoint two kings, Hazael and Jehu, who would be the vehicles of outworking God's wider purpose in the nation. Then he was to find Elisha and anoint him to be his successor as prophet of God to the nation. God also informed him that there were at least another seven thousand people who had not followed the Baals and so were on Elijah's side![12] God saw the bigger picture and wanted

CHAPTER 4   *Supernatural Vs. Spectacular*

Elijah to continue playing his part in the process as his mouthpiece. He wanted him to get on with outworking the naturally supernatural process of his life because in this lay success for him and the nation.

I believe God wants all his people to walk with him in a supernatural process like this. Sometimes what prevents us is the need for an adjustment in our thinking like Elijah had to make, and if that is where this book finds you today, I pray that you will quickly learn the joy of walking with God in a naturally supernatural process as you respond to his gentle whisper in your heart each and every day.

Naaman's Attitude

For some Christians however, there is another problem that has to be dealt with before they can make this adjustment, they have to change their attitude. This was Naaman's problem.

CHAPTER 4   ***Supernatural Vs. Spectacular***

He was the leader of the army of the king of Aram, a mighty warrior and held in high regard, but he had leprosy.[13] At that time it was regarded as a fatal disease; it would slowly eat away his flesh, disfiguring this noble warrior until he was banished from all he loved for fear of cross contagion. His prospects were bad.

Aware of the situation, an Israelite servant girl who served Naaman's wife spoke to her mistress saying, *'If only my master would see the prophet who is in Samaria! He would cure him of his leprosy'.*[14] She was referring to Elisha. Naaman spoke to his king and was granted leave to seek out the man of God. To prepare the way, the king of Aram wrote to the king of Israel asking him to command the prophet to heal the leprosy. He in turn informed Elisha and so the stage was set for a very high-powered encounter. Then we read: *'So Naaman went with his horses and chariots and*

CHAPTER 4   *Supernatural Vs. Spectacular*

stopped at the door of Elisha's house. Elisha sent a messenger to say to him, "Go, wash yourself seven times in the Jordan, and your flesh will be restored and you will be cleansed." [15]

This is not what Naaman was expecting. The prophet did not even come to the door! Instead he sent his servant – a poor substitute in his mind – who suggested he dip in the filthy Jordan river. And why not in the cleaner waters of other rivers he was familiar with? Consequently, '*Naaman went away angry and said, "I thought that he would surely come out to me and stand and call on the name of the LORD his God, wave his hand over the spot and cure me of my leprosy. Are not Abana and Pharpar, the rivers of Damascus, better than any of the waters of Israel? Couldn't I wash in them and be cleansed?" So he turned and went off in a rage.*'[16]

'God wants you to learn to live each day in a supernatural process that embraces all kinds of ordinary things that are actually supernatural in nature and impact'

CHAPTER 4   *Supernatural Vs. Spectacular*

Attitude! His rage was in danger of robbing him of a supernatural intervention simply because it was not spectacular enough for him. Remember, God is naturally supernatural, he does not need to do something spectacular to prove how great he is. In fact he wants you to learn to live each day in a supernatural process that embraces all kinds of ordinary things that are actually supernatural in nature and impact.

Fortunately Naaman was surrounded by some good people who helped him see sense. Away he went and did the 'ordinary thing' which turned out to be quite supernatural and he was healed.

Naaman represents so many in our 21st century church culture, who are similarly convinced that the more severe the problem the more spectacular and eventful the answer has to be. The truth is that Naaman's breakthrough was not just about the event of the Jordan river; it was rooted back home in the

CHAPTER 4 *Supernatural Vs. Spectacular*

process of a relationship with that young Hebrew slave girl. It was she who had first told her mistress about Elisha. So Naaman's breakthrough was relational, his miracle began in his own house, and so will yours. That ordinary and unequal relationship became a supernatural provision to his life.

In the same way, some of you reading this may be looking for a dramatic event while your miracle is in something much closer to hand and perhaps quite ordinary. As we have been seeing, God works primarily through process and the process itself is supernatural. How sad it would be if you allowed a poor attitude to the ordinary things around you, rob you of your miracle. Naaman nearly did, so make sure you don't. Like him, understand that your miracle is more likely to be found rooted in two things: your relationships and your obedience.

> 'Your miracle is more likely to be found rooted in two things: your relationships and your obedience.'

'Determine never to let your attitude prevent your simple obedience to the "gentle whispers" God brings into your life as part of the ongoing process of your Christian life'

CHAPTER 4   *Supernatural Vs. Spectacular*

Sometimes we find it harder to receive through those closest to us, it is easier to go to a conference or seek counsel from a stranger, but God has you in a process. In that process you are surrounded by relationships, your family, friends, pastors and colleagues. Some are old and wise, others young and zealous. Some you know have faults of their own, others are looking to you for guidance and leadership. Whatever the nature of the relationship, please don't discount God's ability to use any of them in the supernatural process of your Christian development. God spoke to Elijah in a whisper and to Naaman through a servant girl, neither were spectacular but both were unexpected and deeply supernatural. So determine never to let your attitude prevent your simple obedience to the 'gentle whispers' God brings into your life as part of the ongoing process of your Christian life.

CHAPTER 4   *Supernatural Vs. Spectacular*

The Supernatural in the Shadows

The book of Esther was almost excluded from inclusion in the Hebrew Scriptures - our Old Testament - because some scholars were concerned that the name of God does not occur in the text. There is no mention of God or the Holy Spirit anywhere in the entire book. Neither is God specifically credited with any of the incredible events recorded in the book.

Yet God is all over this eventful book! Esther describes how God works in the shadows; we find him invisibly at work in the forensic details of an ongoing process behind the visible history-changing events. As such, it is certainly among the most supernatural books in the Bible and yet God is never mentioned.

God's hand in the behind-the-scenes detail is amazing to see. It is evident in the removal of Queen Vashti, in the beauty pageant idea that found Esther who

CHAPTER 4 **Supernatural Vs. Spectacular**

then became the King's favourite, and in the plot to wipe out the Jews by the first ever 'Hitler', a man called Haman. God is in the disturbed sleep of the King who then decided to read some recent history of his own reign, which just *happened* to be the account of how Mordecai exposed an assassination plot against him. We then see God's hand in the King's stated desire to reward Mordecai publicly, which just *happened* to coincide with the arrival of Haman at the palace to ask permission for his genocide plot. On and on it goes until we finally see Haman being hung on the same gallows he had built for Mordecai. God is all over this story!

It was a supernatural process that produced these spectacular events. This is how I believe God works throughout history. History is his-story of supernatural, behind the scenes working of all things together for good. The truth is that if you could dust your life

CHAPTER 4   *Supernatural Vs. Spectacular*

for God's fingerprints, they would be all over you, especially at times when you don't think that God is doing anything in your life because you can't see any visible evidence. The truth is that the God of process continues to work in the shadows of your life whatever events are currently the immediate focus of your life.

Truly Awesome

What is truly awesome? The supernatural process or the spectacular event?

Throughout my time in ministry I have seen a lot of both. I have been to miracle meetings, seen the sick healed and God intervene miraculously in people's lives. I have been used by God in some of these things too. I have laid hands on the sick and seen them recover, prophesied into people's lives, led our

CHAPTER 4   *Supernatural Vs. Spectacular*

church through the 'move of God' associated with Toronto in the 1990s and many of the manifestations and encounters associated with it. I think I have experienced something of the spectacular.

But I have also seen long-standing Christian marriages work through the ups and downs of everyday life – that's supernatural. I've seen businesses grow and succeed that are thoroughly God-centred – that too is supernatural. As I look out across our congregation each time we meet I see black and white, young and old, rich and poor, ex-prostitutes and professors, all doing life together as the people of God, and that is definitely supernatural. When I see teenagers loving God and serving their community, elderly folk encouraging the young to reach higher for God, professional people with their hands in the sink alongside factory workers, students and the disabled – that's what I call supernatural.

CHAPTER 4   *Supernatural Vs. Spectacular*

The truly awesome things about our personal Christian and corporate church lives are those rooted in a supernatural process. Give me those any day over the spectacular events so many have chased. Then, if God in his grace decides that a spectacular encounter is appropriate in my life or church, it is in safe hands because it will be assimilated into the process and not over endorsed so much that we end up putting our lives on hold until the next one comes along.

In the supernatural versus spectacular contest, supernatural is the winner every time!

CHAPTER 4 *Supernatural Vs. Spectacular*

[1] Romans 1:17
[2] Hebrews 11:1
[3] 1 Kings 18
[4] 1 Kings 19:2
[5] 1 Kings 18:22 and 40
[6] 1 Kings 18:21
[7] 1 Kings 19:3
[8] 1 Kings 19:9
[9] 1 Kings 19:11-12
[10] 1 Kings 19:12
[11] 1 Kings 19:15
[12] 1 Kings 19:15-18
[13] 2 Kings 5:1
[14] 2 Kings 5:3
[15] 2 Kings 5:9-10
[16] 2 Kings 5:11-12

'The truly awesome things about our personal Christian and corporate church lives are those rooted in a supernatural process. Give me those any day over the spectacular events so many have chased'

'I have encouraged you to live 'process based Christianity' which does not mean ignoring the events in your life, they must be assimilated into the process and there they find their place of maximum impact'

CHAPTER 5

Foundational Choices

The more we explore the relationship between events and process, the more we are understanding the need to have a healthy balance between the two in our lives. It is not a matter of embracing one or the other, it is all about understanding how they work together and us not putting too much emphasis in the wrong place. I have encouraged you to live 'process based Christianity' which does not mean ignoring the events in your life, they must be assimilated into the process and there they find their place of maximum impact. And I am confident that if you start to live 'process based Christianity' you will thrive!

CHAPTER 5 **Foundational Choices**

Contrasting Foundations

This is a foundational concept. So much so that when you consider what Jesus taught about building on a proper foundation, the contrast between events and process once again jumps off the page.

Jesus had just spent an extended period teaching the crowd from a mountainside – we call it the Sermon on the Mount. He started in Matthew 5:1 and taught some of his most profound truths, things like: the Beatitudes, how we should be salt and light, and the fact that he had not come to abolish the law and prophets but to fulfil them. He reinterpreted aspects of the law, taught them to love their enemies and to give to the needy. Then he taught them how to pray, leaving them the Lord's Prayer as a model. He then moved onto fasting, living a worry-free life, seeking first God's Kingdom and being careful not to judge others. He taught them about asking his Father for

CHAPTER 5   **Foundational Choices**

good gifts and how they should treat others as they would like to be treated themselves. He taught them that a tree is recognised by its fruit, be it good or bad. Finally, Jesus drew all this amazing teaching together into one simple concluding thought:

'Therefore everyone who hears these words of mine and puts them into practice is like a wise man who built his house on the rock. The rain came down, the streams rose, and the winds blew and beat against that house; yet it did not fall, because it had its foundation on the rock. But everyone who hears these words of mine and does not put them into practice is like a foolish man who built his house on sand. The rain came down, the streams rose, and the winds blew and beat against that house, and it fell with a great crash.'[1]

What an event that sermon had been! So much profound, life-changing truth had been imparted to the listeners. No wonder Matthew goes on to observe

CHAPTER 5 **_Foundational Choices_**

that, *'When Jesus had finished saying these things, the crowds were amazed at his teaching'.*[2] They could forever after tell their friends and family that they were there, they heard Jesus teach those life-changing things. But the big question would really be, did it make a difference to them individually?

The Sermon on the Mount is the ancient equivalent of a present day conference or simply sitting under the anointed teaching that your faithful pastor imparts to you each week. It is an event but has it affected your foundations? As Jesus explained, everything you hear contributes to the building process of your Christian life, and what it is built on is absolutely essential. Is it built on a foundation of *'hearing these words of mine and putting them into practice'?* If so, each piece of teaching is being integrated into the developing process of your Christian life. If, however, you sit there week after week saying 'amen' and nodding your head in agreement but never actually applying,

'It will take a future event to expose whether or not you are actually living your life as a God-centered daily process. That event will be a storm'

CHAPTER 5 **Foundational Choices**

outworking or doing the Word that is taught, you are like the foolish man who built the house of his life on sand.

Only time will tell. It will take a future event to expose whether or not you are actually living your life as a God-centered daily process. That event will be a storm. When it hits, you will be shaken to your foundation and just what is in there will be exposed. If you are living 'event based Christianity' the storm will dominate and take over your life; it will explain why spiritually you have no reserves for a time like this. You will justify yourself and be side-lined from effective Christian growth and service for however long it takes for this event to be replaced by the next. But if you are living 'process based Christianity' this storm-event will be taken in your stride, integrated into the bigger process of your life and your progress maintained.

CHAPTER 5 **Foundational Choices**

The storm is never to blame when the building of your life collapses, it is always the state of the foundations that must be examined. A foundation of 'hearing and doing' as part of living a 'process based Christian life' will always prove to be rock-like; solid, secure, certain, immovable, unshakeable. But a foundation of hearing without an active process of doing will always be fragile, uncertain, insecure, shaky and unable to take the weight of the storm.

James, who was the half brother of Jesus, and so had grown up with him, heard him teach and seen the quality of his life, made a similar observation about the Christian life. He wrote, *'Do not merely listen to the word, and so deceive yourselves. Do what it says. Anyone who listens to the word but does not do what it says is like a man who looks at his face in a mirror and, after looking at himself, goes away and immediately forgets what he looks like. But the man who looks intently*

'When it rains, what's in the ground just grows! The event is just revealing who you are, so don't blame the rain or the storm'

CHAPTER 5   **_Foundational Choices_**

into the perfect law that gives freedom, and continues to do this, not forgetting what he has heard, but doing it— he will be blessed in what he does.'[3]

As we have stressed throughout this book, all the power is in the process and all the blessing is in the process. If you want to be 'blessed in what you do' as James states, you must be a doer of God's Word, and doing is a process. Make sure it is an integral part of your Christian foundation because the storm-like events in your life will simply expose what your foundations are made of. Or, to think of it another way, when it rains, what's in the ground just grows! The event is just revealing who you are, so don't blame the rain or the storm.

Neither should we blame the church, our family, friends or other external factors. In the final analysis we have to make a personal decision to live a 'process based' Christian life.

CHAPTER 5 *Foundational Choices*

The Tale of Two Gods

Sadly, the wider church does not necessarily help us in this choice. The very fact that many are living what I have called 'event based Christianity' is testimony itself to a worldview held by many across the Christian community today. And my teaching in this book will find itself in opposition to those who hold such an 'event based' view of their lives, the way God works and therefore the available solutions. Unfortunately this leaves you, the individual Christian, receiving mixed signals about the best way to approach and develop your Christian life.

I would even go so far as to say that many Christians appear to have two Gods, *a local church God* and a *conference God*. The difference between the two is the difference between 'event based Christianity' and 'process based Christianity'. The local church God speaks with the language of process but the conference

CHAPTER 5   **Foundational Choices**

God just 'zaps' people as an event. The local church God speaks about growing up, taking responsibility for our own lives and choices, while the conference God just lays hands on us and prophesies us into our call and anointing. The local church God is like a father, the conference God is like Father Christmas. The local church God sends me home to work it out, the conference God often calls me away from home into the pursuit of my ministry.

I don't want to be too sweeping in my statements here or over generalise things, but this has certainly been a common issue in my experience as a church leader over the past thirty years. It is like a child who asks its dad for extra pocket money. When he refuses, the child moves on to grandad and asks him for the money. And this is of course all done in the hope that they never talk to each other about it! However, it all falls apart when the child discovers that both 'dads' are onto their game and both say 'no'.

'There's one God and he's committed to both the wisdom of process and the power of events that strengthen the process'

CHAPTER 5 **_Foundational Choices_**

Many restless believers, weary of process, travel half way around the world to a conference hoping to hear what they want to hear. However, when they suddenly find themselves listening to exactly the same things that their local pastor back at home has been saying for months, they begin to realise that the God of the local church and the God of the conference are actually the same God. There's one God, he's not divided like Dad and Grandad, and he's committed to both the wisdom of process and the power of events that strengthen the process. So, if what we hear at the conference doesn't inspire us to continue in our commitment to process, and doesn't send us into our local communities to outwork it, this is probably a conference we don't need.

CHAPTER 5 **_Foundational Choices_**

Clarifying the Choices

I have made a case in this book for living the only way I believe God intended us to live. This involves a relational process; a walk with God that takes daily steps towards outworking his will for our lives and reaching our destiny. My life is a testimony to living 'process based Christianity' as are the lives of countless others in my home church and across the wider Body of Christ. I believe all the true success stories you will read about have approached their Christianity this way. But the competition is out there!

After all, how can we who counsel from our 'process based Christianity' regarding, say someone's financial problems, ever hope to compete with the visiting preacher who is declaring people debt free every night in his exciting and eventful services? Or how can our counsel to change your habits in order to change your life compete with the instant deliverance

CHAPTER 5 **Foundational Choices**

on offer across town? How can our appeal for a daily process of self-control compete with the 'casting out of the demon that's making me do it' that's on offer in 'Brother Fix It's' meetings? For those who are living 'event based Christianity' it never can. Their ever present need for another event to fix the problem, make them feel good again, confirm God's will and assure them of their anointing will always make them grasp the event for that elusive 'quick fix'.

It deeply concerns me that promise-filled events like these do damage to our testimony as God's people. What kind of signal does it send to the church in a city, when a brother under the process of discipline in one church gets offered a job in another church just because they laid hands on him and zapped him back into ministry? I reckon that our commitment to think and work in a long-term process and so influence how things get done, seems dull and unbelieving to the 'all we need is a revival' crowd.

CHAPTER 5   *Foundational Choices*

Similarly, our teaching that your breakthrough is about 'generational choices' can't compete with what many prefer to believe; which is that they can't help their behaviour, because it's caused by the generational curses from their ancestry.

And I could go on! There are certainly two worldviews out there, one founded on living the Christian life as a process and another based on living it as a series of events. But as Jesus said, *'by their fruit you will recognise them.'*[4]

Beware Uncle Joe

As kids we used to have an uncle called Joe. When Uncle Joe visited our house he was our hero. He gave us sweets, money, toys, piggyback rides and even the occasional drag on his cigarette. Uncle Joe never once corrected us, disciplined us or refused us anything. In short, Uncle Joe was our parent's worst nightmare!

CHAPTER 5 **Foundational Choices**

Many itinerant ministries are the 'Uncle Joes' of church life and any local church pastors who are intolerant of process are no better. Disconnected from the reality and responsibility of the process of local church, some preachers breeze into our towns and cities with a 'one night stand' mentality. During their meetings they promise the earth to our local church children, many of whom are already frustrated by their pastor's latest counsel to take responsibility and work things through. They then come home from Uncle Joe's meeting spoilt and unwilling to embrace the process of growth that is the blessing of those who are planted in God's House. Uncle Joe prophesies greatness over our children then sends them back home to us, their spiritual parents, who are now expected to cash the blank cheque which Uncle Joe gave them. I've got a better idea, if Uncle Joe thinks so much of them why doesn't he adopt them and raise them up into the spiritual giants he believes they are!

CHAPTER 5 **Foundational Choices**

I don't want to offend Uncle Joe but would like to say something very heartfelt to him: 'Uncle Joe, we love you, we appreciate your ministry and anointing, but you are not helping us to grow responsible children or churches. You are undermining process and exaggerating events. You are confused between the supernatural and the spectacular and are confusing our local church kids in the process too. Uncle Joe, can we make a deal, that if you will add the balance and beauty of process to your ministry then we will gladly send our kids over to your place and would probably invite you over to ours more often too.'

'Uncle Joe, we love you, we appreciate your ministry and anointing, but you are not helping us to grow responsible children or churches.'

CHAPTER 5   *Foundational Choices*

Case Closed

I rest my case. The Christian life is a process not an event and if you will live it as such, you will be blessed, fruitful and fulfilled.

In my introduction I described the contrast between 'event based Christianity' and 'process based Christianity' which we have explored in this book, as being one of the most important principles I have ever taught. Putting pen to paper has only served to reinforce my view. This teaching is absolutely crucial to our success as God's people in this generation and for every future one.

CHAPTER 5 **Foundational Choices**

My prayer is that as you have read and thought about your own particular world-view as a believer, this teaching has empowered you to make some fundamental changes to your perspective. The evidence will ultimately be clear for all to see and maybe this short book will help you explain yourself to those who try to understand the changes they see in you. You have simply moved from living 'event based Christianity' to living life as a God-centred process into which every event of your life is seamlessly integrated.

CHAPTER 5 **_Foundational Choices_**

This principle is indeed like a quiet child amongst a boisterous family; it gets little attention because it doesn't shout the loudest. But having spoken up for this quiet child I hope that you will now join me in saying to all the noisy attention-grabbing kids, 'Be quiet!' because this quiet child really does have something important to say.

---

[1] Matthew 7:24-27
[2] Matthew 7:28
[3] James 1:22-25
[4] Matthew 7:20

'There are certainly two world-views out there, one founded on living the Christian life as a process and another based on living it as a series of events. But as Jesus said, "by their fruit you will recognise them"'

Full details of other resources by
Paul Scanlon are available from:

Abundant Life Church
Wapping Road, Bradford
West Yorkshire BD3 0EQ

Tel: +44 (0)1274 307233
Fax: +44 (0)1274 740698
Email: admin@alm.org.uk

For a copy of our free quarterly magazine
'Voice to the Nations' please contact us as above.

Visit our online store at www.alm.org.uk

Browse the full range of preaching, teaching, training, music
and worship resources available from Abundant Life Ministries.

*Other book titles available from
Abundant Life Resources:*

It's Not Over 'Till The Barren Woman Sings
by Paul Scanlon

Crossing Over
by Paul Scanlon

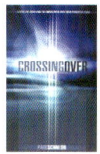

Consumer or Consumed?
by Charlotte Scanlon-Gambill

The Battle for the Loins
by Paul Scanlon

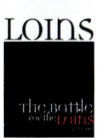